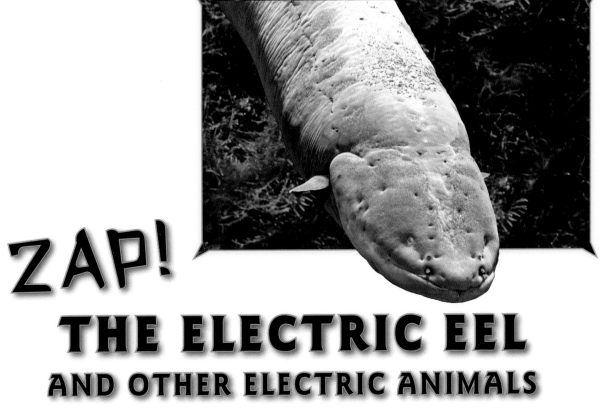

ZAP!
THE ELECTRIC EEL
AND OTHER ELECTRIC ANIMALS

Greg Roza

PowerKiDS press.

New York

Published in 2011 by The Rosen Publishing Group, Inc.
29 East 21st Street, New York, NY 10010

First Edition

Editor: Jennifer Way
Book Design: Kate Laczynski

Photo Credits: Cover, pp. 1, 20–21 George Grall/Getty Images; p. 4 Ken Lucas/Getty Images; pp. 5, 18 Shutterstock.com; p. 6 Timm Schamberger/AFP/Getty Images; p. 7 © 2006 Steven G. Johnson and donated to Wikipedia under GFDL and CC-by-SA/http://en.wikipedia.org/wiki/File:Electric-eel.jpg; pp. 8–9, 13 (bottom), 16–17 © Leszczynski, Zigmund/Animals Animals; p. 10 David Wrobel/Getty Images; p. 11 © Matthias Kleine/ http://en.wikipedia.org/wiki/File:Torpedo_fuscomaculata2.jpg; pp. 13 (top), 15 Hemera/ Thinkstock; p. 14 © OSF/Hall, Howard/Animals Animals; p. 19 Jeff Rotman/Getty Images; p. 22 Gordon Wiltsie/Getty Images.

Library of Congress Cataloging-in-Publication Data

Roza, Greg.
  Zap! : the electric eel and other electric animals / by Greg Roza. — 1st ed.
    p. cm. — (Armed and dangerous)
Includes index.
ISBN 978-1-4488-2547-9 (library binding) — ISBN 978-1-4488-2678-0 (pbk.) —
ISBN 978-1-4488-2679-7 (6-pack)
1. Electric fishes—Juvenile literature. 2. Electric organs in fishes—Juvenile literature.
3. Animal defenses—Juvenile literature. I. Title.
  QL639.1.R69 2011
  591.47—dc22

                                          2010023589

Manufactured in the United States of America

CPSIA Compliance Information: Batch #WW11PK: For Further Information contact Rosen Publishing, New York, New York at 1-800-237-9932

CONTENTS

IT'S ELECTRIC

Animals have many ways of hunting **prey** and guarding themselves against **predators**. Some have sharp teeth and claws. Others have special shapes or colors that allow them to hide in plain sight. Still others use **poison**. A few very special animals are armed with electricity!

The electric animals in this book are all **marine** animals. You have likely heard of the

This is an electric eel. It is one of the world's best-known electric animals.

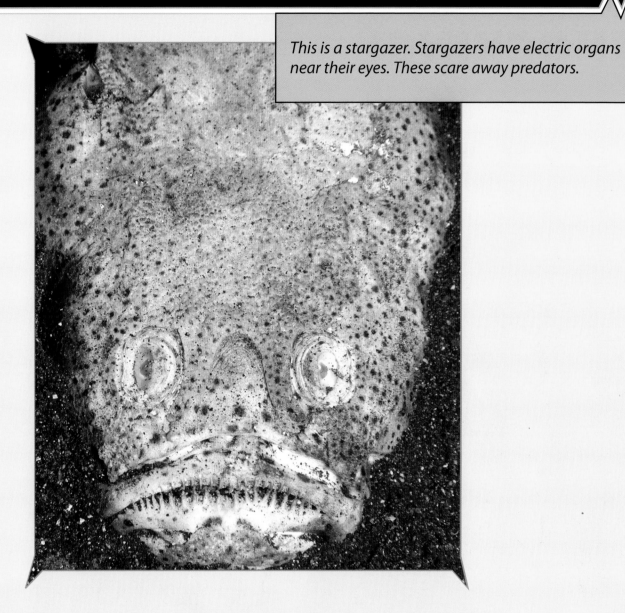

This is a stargazer. Stargazers have electric organs near their eyes. These scare away predators.

electric eel, but there are many other shocking fish in the sea! This book will show you these animals and explain how these armed and dangerous animals make and use electricity.

SHOCKING!

Have you ever walked across a rug, touched a doorknob, and felt a shock? That zap you felt is called static electricity. Some electric fish can give a more powerful shock than static electricity.

This machine is sending electricity into this woman's body and making her hair stand on end.

Each **species** of electric fish uses its electricity in different ways. Some shock to kill their prey. Other electric fish use their power to shock to scare away predators that get too close. Still others send out electric signals to talk with other fish of their species. There are even fish that use their electricity to find their way in dark or muddy water.

ELECTRIC CELLS

Plants and animals are made up of tiny building blocks called cells. Groups of cells that work together to do a job make up body parts called **organs**.

Electric fish have organs that work a bit as batteries do. Instead of making electricity with batteries, electric fish make their electricity in special organs.

These organs are made up of flat cells that are grouped on top of and next to each other. The cells make electricity from **chemical energy** that is stored within the cells. In some animals, such as the electric eel, the electricity made by these organs is strong enough to kill their prey!

STRONG AND WEAK

There are two kinds of shocks that electric animals can make. Fish that use electricity to hunt are called strongly electric. These fish can shock strongly enough to stun their prey. Some fish can even kill their prey by shocking it.

Fish that do not use their electricity for hunting are called weakly electric. Some weakly electric fish make

The glass knife fish, shown above, is a weakly electric animal.

an electric field around themselves. These electric fields are like clouds of electricity. They can use these electric fields to talk with other fish. These fields can also bounce off objects so that the fish can sense where these objects are in the water.

ELECTRIC EELS

Amazon River

South America

The electric eel is not a true eel, even though it looks like other eels. The electric eel is a type of knife fish. It lives in the Amazon River, in South America. The electric eel uses a strong electric shock to stun small animals, such as fish, crabs, shrimp, and even small mammals. The electric eel does not have any teeth, so it eats its prey whole!

The Amazon River is the second-longest river in the world. Electric eels are found throughout this river, mostly on the muddy bottom and in places where the water flows slowly.

Electric eels eat fish, such as the discus fish shown here.

Electric eels have three pairs of organs that they use to make electricity. These organs make up most of the eel's weight and length.

The three pairs of organs that electric eels use to make electricity are called the Main organ, the Hunter's organ, and the Sach's organ.

ELECTRIC RAYS

There are 14 species of electric rays that live around the world. Rays have wide, flat bodies. Electric rays are strongly electric and can stun prey or escape predators.

Electric rays are slow-moving fish that live on the ocean floor.

Clams are mollusks, one of the kinds of animals that electric rays eat.

There are two main kinds of electric rays. The first group is made up of larger animals such as the coffin ray. These electric rays stun bony fish, **mollusks**, **crustaceans**, and worms and then swallow them whole. The other group is made up of smaller electric rays, such as the numbfish. These smaller rays stun and eat prey that live near the bottom of the ocean.

KNIFE FISH

There are more than 60 species of knife fish. They live in rivers in Central and South America. However, unlike the electric eel, which is also a knife fish, most knife fish cannot shock their prey to stun them.

Most knife fish are weakly electric. They use electricity to sense objects in the

water around them. Knife fish have very bad eyesight, so putting out these electric fields let them see in the water. When prey enters their electric fields, they can tell where it is, its shape, and its size. Knife fish can even use their electric fields to talk to other knife fish!

STARGAZERS

This stargazer is burying itself in the sand.

Stargazers live in the Atlantic Ocean along the coast from North Carolina in North America all the way down to northern South America. Stargazers get their name because their eyes are on top of their heads. When they hide themselves in the sand, they can look up from their hiding places. When prey swims overhead, the stargazer comes out of its hiding place and eats it.

The stargazer's electric organs are behind its eyes. These organs are weakly electric. The stargazer uses electricity to scare away larger fish that might want to eat it.

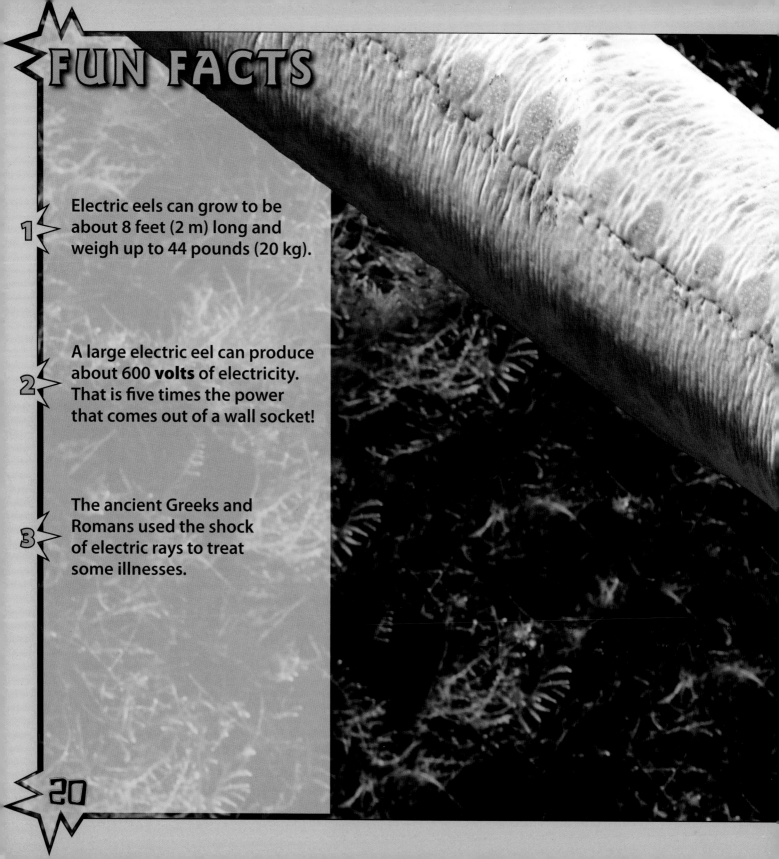

FUN FACTS

1 Electric eels can grow to be about 8 feet (2 m) long and weigh up to 44 pounds (20 kg).

2 A large electric eel can produce about 600 **volts** of electricity. That is five times the power that comes out of a wall socket!

3 The ancient Greeks and Romans used the shock of electric rays to treat some illnesses.

Knife fish get their name from the shape of their bodies. 4

Stargazers' colors blend in with their surroundings. They use their fins to hide themselves in sand. Then they shock smaller fish that swim by. 5

The short-nose electric ray is the smallest electric ray. It measures just 4 inches (10 cm) across. 6

ELECTRIC FISH AND PEOPLE

Electric fish do not often attack people. Sometimes they shock a person who is swimming or wading in waters where an electric eel or ray is resting.

The shock of an electric eel is strong, but it generally is not deadly. However, people have drowned after being

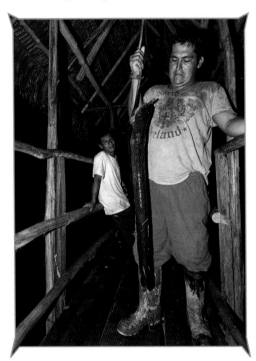

stunned. People have also been killed by several shocks from a group of electric eels. In most cases, electric fish are not a big danger to people. Some of these shocking fish, such as the black ghost knife fish, are even kept as pets!

GLOSSARY

chemical energy (KEH-mih-kul EH-ner-jee) Power made from a reaction between two things.

crustaceans (krus-TAY-shunz) Animals that have no backbones and have hard shells and live mostly in water.

marine (muh-REEN) Having to do with the sea.

mollusks (MAH-lusks) Animals without backbones and with soft bodies and, often, shells.

organs (OR-genz) Parts inside bodies that do jobs.

poison (POY-zun) To cause pain or death with matter made by an animal's body.

predators (PREH-duh-terz) Animals that kill other animals for food.

prey (PRAY) An animal that is hunted by another animal for food.

species (SPEE-sheez) One kind of living thing. All people are one species.

volts (VOHLTS) Units for measuring electricity.

INDEX

WEB SITES

Due to the changing nature of Internet links, PowerKids Press has developed an online list of Web sites related to the subject of this book. This site is updated regularly. Please use this link to access the list:
www.powerkidslinks.com/armd/zap/